night audit

brian waksmunski

this is dedicated to downtown Oakland
and San Francisco's Tenderloin

100% of the author's profits from the
sale of this collection will be donated
to local organizations focused on the
faces of those scenes, beginning with
Larkin Street Youth Services

also by brian:
The Pirates of Ipanema
The Mojito Hustle

special thanks to Hotel Kabuki in Japantown,
SF, where these were composed in those
precious quiet moments between late-night
check-ins and early morning check-outs

contents

ateasive

werewolf me with your
howlin fangs
stomp my shine by hyphy dance
lap the sweat that
beads my bangs
credit check my power stance
gauntlet beat god radar blips
post with haste
my soul sent stamps
puff the pipe with pastor lips
invest faith not in moonlit lamps
number your neurons
alphabetically please
we wanna be tight
with the tit-twisting blame
hark how they billy'd
the goat for the cheese
replay how we O.J.'d
the chief with the dame
swim for the swami
with crystal unclouded

unhook the hung hat
of the pontiff perceived
flash me a badge
and I'll ticket your circus
flower the caskets
of futures bereaved
prepare bloody rare
the Tenderloin tips
buyer beware
the stock of the streets
padlock the chastity belt
'round the hips
grind up the key
with the Space Burger meats
tongue tie the Tribune town crier
muzzle the muckraker media sluts
tumble dry low the Valhalla denier
cock-block creationist
ark-building nuts
cash the masseuse
with a lotioned-palm slap
green card your midnight
Skype call to Manila
encourage the Curry
barrage with a clap
handcuff your kid
to an endangered gorilla
hijack a tug

from the pier to the port
castrate the cranes
so they can't multiply
compost a conex of silent support
recycle your most polite
putdown reply
Miranda right self-righteousness
quid pro quo
the concept respect
conscience-cam
thy neighbor less
rent control your rank expect
then tango solo
'cross the bridge of the bay
to alcatraz celled inhibitions
sequoia proudly
each pawn took play
and wiki not dead definitions

catch-44

fading blanco ornamental
hollow symbol castle
comes complete with furnished office
bumper-seated throne
relocation retrospected
hardly worth the hastle
departure date inflexible
no option rent to own
potential buzzed by promises
clean carpeted arrival
surprised to see a mutiny
before the ship left port
confused to watch the seeds of hope
sprout trees of hate revival
while career clowns coordinate
to your ambitions thwart
your favorite suit
sewn from a naive thread
philosophy forged carefully
from out of cannon tomes
thin optimism

like a snakeskin shed
as protesters stoked fires
in a hundred separate Romes
the guidon bearers
cowardly broke rank
dividing and professing
demographic-polled convictions
you stretched between them
bridge-like as a plank
pleading against patria derelictions
the mosaic painted on the ceiling
of the halls of power
is nothing but a mirror image
of the bold who look
now you stand atop the Mount
and sense the waning hour
aware the fires of history
were not given but took
therein lies your prism-painted rubix
what future profs will coin
"catch forty-four"
the currency of promise
bought your tickets
but there's no one to collect them
by the brighter future door
the handle is not made of brass
but plaster
the peep hole too high fastened

and quite small
your touch reveals the breadth
of the disaster
the door is just a painting on a wall
so you turn to face again
your loyal fellowship
noting the last embers
of impatience in their eyes
as the clowns slip you
a card of lifetime membership
lighting cigars to celebrate
survival of the guise
you have the skill to scale the wall
and solitary summit
though you alone will see
the other side
you have the strength to smash a hole
and blast a passage from it
but victim costs from brick debris
your conscience won't abide
a thousand puddles dot
the land divided
darkened pools of sentiments
diverged beyond repair
drawn together as a wave one-minded
their crest could breach the wall
with space to spare
with this your dream

you pulpit plea for union
though from the Mount
your voice begins to strain
and the crowd reverts to conflict
from communion
as your final sunlit hour starts to wane

woakland

sunstar rises shaded over woakland
west coast casual no notion late
blondie cracks deposits
in the joke fund
inciting one more
who's/to/blame debate
hipster smiles still wrapped
in package plastic
celebratants from one trick towns
east zone
pilgrimaging silicon monastics
tattoo masked/ coordinated tones
searching algorithms
for meaning of life links
weeding out the tangents
from the florals
subjugating cravings to dietary kinks
retro-fit with second hand
bought morals
demographic deck two time
cut/the/cut trick shufflers
new suits without a card below a ten
dealers tuck their tips
like pole dance hustlers

and triple time the ante
with a platinum-plated grin
keep the pace
or place your stuff in storage
anticipate the quake
or disappear between the cracks
buffet by way of midday
dumpster forage
retirement by lay on railroad tracks
professional protestors paid per hour
rent a megaphone for extra fee
volume more than purpose
lung the crier
slogan scribes for hire root the tree
officers only honored
at city sanctioned 'rades
impromptu expressions
exclusively anti-establishment
with every accusation
faith in fairness further fades
anarchists blow their told/you/so's
to rally brother banishment
mayor's got a parrot for a spokesman
two tongued with silver fittings
for a beak
pressboys origami facts from fiction
but blondie's on a four day
boycott streak

gather by the water
on picnic blanket patches
no traffic for the roll and smoke
commute
critter gaze and marvel
at the variance of batches
opine sans provocation
on the deity dispute
the glass cased Grand cathedral
dares the stoners to indulge
though vandalism scratches
are insured
so they pass a signed petition
for the clergy to divulge
their authorship of insurrection stirred
the broadway/ twelfth street
beat patrol
is never disappointed
though company there kept
is best kept salted
brash barkers man their posts
like knights anointed
while the lucky half
cast lots for debts defaulted
the off the grid delinquents
mind their manners
while off the clock protectors
cash their chips

hot tubs steam too discreet
for proof demanders
at addresses unmarked
against loose lips
the moonrock warns
the hourglass forsaken
countdown of shadow coverage
for the vamps
first glint of sunstar
stowaways awaken
disinterested in clouds
beyond their camps
mad cyclists race wild
down international
lamenting lack of prescribed
medications
spewing blue-laced tirades
barely graspable
doomsdaying further withdrawal
implications
the royals loiter freely in the courtyard
bus stop benches perma occupied
shaded sidewalk
slated for the vanguard
muni organizers bona fide
seasons shift with subtle
breeze inflections

audit

while palm readers on backpage
predict what the wind portends
as benchwarmers brace
for further dream defections
and blondie racks the focus of her lens

potluck hues

tragedy of a bargain
civic plaza morning market
planted in a pot/ centered
watered in that pot/ nurtured
strategic strung to guide the growth
elegantly curved
unlike the wild ones random lurching
framing edges of raw forest
reminding at a glance
of flirtatious waxing sophist
in passing unexpected overheard
"I'd rather be a flower than a florist"
prefer to be a poem than a poet
blaring note than a brassy horn
stench of a scent
than formulated fragrance
fresh dew than bending grass blades
genuflecting to the morn
proud to be a weed instead of orchid
rebellious punk disruptor
host resented
invading unabashedly
a crevice of my choosing
poisoned/ plucked/ sheared

swift removed but unrepented
not the lion but the roar
that shakes the soul's savannah
not the water but the wet
which floods hope valley basin
not the eagle but the flight
amid the clouds of crazy
not the medal but the triumph
at olympics of high treason
sweetness not the sugar
brilliance not the star
warmth not the fire
sadness not the war
ethereal yearnings foolish as prayer
objectful of the tangible
futile as prostration
envious of the experience
of immediate sensation
frustrated by the filters unsuspendable
the process underangeable
do not order me to flower
for the light as restitution
tax collectors buzzing
rabid nectar contribution
closed petals as pursed lips
at ends of roots
muscling ever deeper in the dirt
not disoriented nor ignorant

to bio-law pursuits
bittered by the logic
disturbed by the design
spitefully inspired
ever darker down the mine
while bees above revile
the absent fruit atop the vine
/
plastic clay ceramic stone
not every flower pot the same
common theme restricted zone
design depends on crapshoot claim
unspoken truth by gardener known
even the stone cannot contain
determined roots rebellious sown
from seeds detestful of restrain
beyond the random chance of case
elemental matters reign
necessities depend on grace
by light or lamp by hose or rain
before the roots can well rebel
before the bloom can pot arraign
the planted seedlings helpless dwell
awaiting Fortune's fate campaign
many seeds underfed
with stems stunted
many weeds pulled in acts
labeled "progress"

audit

misdeed imprints
from pale thumbs unwanted
late-to-blooms last in line
for the largesse
but to dream for transplant
is proof of the fool
to wilt to the pot circumstance
a life fail
to bloom and bloom better
the singular rule
to fait accompli an emotional bail
there was beauty
before there were florists
unprotected by pots
from the whim of the land
still some rares grow unspoilt in
uncataloged forests
far from wrath of the spade and cruel
reach of the hand
redwood of a spirit in daffodil caste
such is the lot of the lucky who thrives
soon as the bloom
the season forecast turns
and the moment to reseed arrives
the risk to be trodden
or otherwise snuffed
by a paw or a shoe or a bicycle tire
adds a sprinkle of thrill

to the urbanite life
that can pass at the pace
of an off the bay zephyr
but better a month in a park
by the lake
than a year by a lamp in a pot
more righteous by breeze
shall my soulseeds freebreak
than by bouquet
my destiny bought

lake merrittocracy

east bay eggs roll hard on the boil
graffiti sprayed silver and black
long gone mama goose served
with waffles side order
rough to the touch
with scarred shells
chipped and cracked
a lake for a face to identi-empower
better not to imbibe the free water
though they that true thirst
don't discriminate drink
as the boat that can't float
don't discriminate sink
while the wildlife wait gathered
for stale bread providers
and wonder why ancestors
fished for their dinners
/
four biblical extras
encountered while walking
four chances four choices
four mirrors four tests
I prepare my straight stare
and tune eardrums for pleas

paced on rhythm of jingle
of pocketed keys
nothing too spareable
nothing too needed
four quarters in change
for the night unbetrothed
I finger their ridges
and guess at their stories
the purses they've ported
the sins they've resorted
lost tickets they've scratched
good fortune they've flipped
loads they've rinse cycled
and coffee shops tipped
/
lizard the lean
works the circuit eighteenth
the lucky's the pho spot
the baggy's and walgreens
he slips back and forth
from one side to the other
as he spies saints on errands
and hustles to offer
thin arms for load labor
at karma based rate
but I've nothing to carry
or feeling of tire
and his casual cadence

audit

shades shy of strait dire
I deny his petition of need
without slowing
he too on the move
had asked already knowing
our daily routine of one wanting
both going
/
beatle on BART
with his bum strung guitar
last ghost of the lonely hearts
club scene
strums and howls
as the rails banshee backup
swimming under the bay
like a grey submarine
"I'm the walrus" he claims
"and I play for my son"
as he plucks and he pulls at the
instrument's strings
his bucket flows full
by the time the song's done
"may a peaceful night pay well
a refund" he sings
with his charm and his polish
and talent-won rent
he gimps from the car
at the embarcadero

top one percent
of the base one percent
with half of my coins
in his pile of dinheiro
/
not so much to the wind
or the chill but the dark
Red the hen has a manic aversion
to night
so she diners and lobbies
and bus lines about
with two two gallon purses
clutched by the straps tight
curly hair ever bowed
winter coat ever on
she chases the morning
til catches the dawn
then benches and parks
and solar revives
til the cycle completes
and the black threat arrives
creeps nonchalant
to a chair in the corner
struggling steady across the tiled floor
not yearning for change
but a respite of quarter
for a minute to minute
to one minute more

audit

hands clasped and eyes closed
she resembles my mother
the hour is late and the lobby is vacant
yet I nudge her awake her
and exit door take her
lest a guest be aghast
at the sight of a vagrant
/
sidewalk starfish
splayed wide on Larkin
perks at the scent
from my pork bahn mi
posture of buddha with zen scoliosis
accepts smoke donations but not EBT
sarcastically thanks those
who don't seem to notice
camouflaged by the context
of Tenderloin trash
like a petal of pink on the lip of a lotus
or a tower of babble
in town balderdash
same gender same age
same all the breaks tone
woe be done to the one
who thine own self denies
I thumb flick a quarter
as sympathy shown
though it more my good luck

than goodwill implies
/
as I pass by the lake
on my night's final leg
the morning commuters
and joggers
share lanes
the geese grass their breakfast
like unioned groundskeepers
and hiss into motion
late-waking lawn sleepers
who shakedown the bins
in dream famished pursuit
of the downtown beat version
of low hanging fruit
while my still unspent coin
tries to reason evoke
from the random rulebook
at the yoke of the Oak

black lightning

begrudge the sunlight
influence on sight
blaring bright rays blindfold blocking
boundaries of perception
but Lady Universe
performs her striptease in the night
to the restless unquenched
questioner's delight
/

a telescope positioned well conditions
right will space enhance
a microscope and petri dish
detail expose clues missed by glance
in darkened hall a tricky task
from wall to floor the flower dance
in alley back smoke rocket fuel to
lightspeed jump the mind expanse
at touch the cheek feels warm and soft
despite the August evening chill
her laugh sounds nervous out of depth
uneased among the unfamiliar
city girl or so she thought
with address high atop Nob Hill
unmarked by map now finds herself

where late night joints will not deliver
rooftop perched on Hotel Hartland
following the smoke he looks
skyward guessing constellations
unrecalled from long-shelved books
unimpressed he then descends
to where dim lamps ignore the nooks
where owlish eyes like zippos burn
their lighthouse beacons
warning/ calling/ daring
modern Lews and Clarks to find
their private northwest route
unblazeable while Helios
awashes all the eyes can see
deceptive tease of foottrod trails
a shellgame short the hunted pea
not sight but lost the sense
most critical to read the legend key
not bright but blocked the role
preferred for solar flares
that burst esprit
as dusk hints close
break fast your camp
and leave behind
what can't be carried
drop dead weight of doom predicts
and carcass discard fears unburied
when the night has fallen full

and dangers rustle nearby brush
inhale two-lunged the scent unknown
embrace complete that danger rush
wait not for ground of solid rock
before you into darkness step
waste not time for flying high
on walkthrough drills for landing prep
celebrate not guarantees
but genuine mind blown surprise
know you're close to cliff edge sought
when certainties destabilize
near to rocks daredevil dives
confident in wax-glued wings
birds on bridge with nods applaud
as arms spread wide
she airborne sings
peaceful smiles and swiftly soars
as mercy wind last second lifts
cosmic reward for reckless risk
her flight fate fortune shifts
spinning round in search of peaks
or landmarks sure to recognize
he slips down slope on gravel loose
howl cursing "not-my-fault" demise
the night ignores the weakling's cries
and mocks the gambler's
chance despair
don't roll the rocks across the felt

if weight of loss backbone can't bear
nor enter night with torch ablaze
and auth. experience impair
nor morn excite as rays return
and stifle inner trapped Voltaire

/

I survey the gaps between the starlight
for twinkles from ships
yet to cross the abyss
Pheidippides messengers fleet footing
secrets to color the void
and inform the amiss
past the horizon
where black lightning strikes
in concert with thunder
that rumbles my soul
outside of the spectrum
the kodachrome captures
where patterns kaleid
beyond Painter's control
I spur the beast 'neath me
to galloping speed
and we breakneck across the terrain
we'll circle the hills and hurdle the
streams with be-damned disregard
for the meteor rain
charging the storm with the fiendish
intent of summoning bolts

from clouds blown in drifts
until that black lightning grants our
request and blesses the effort
with heaven-sent gifts
I search for singed earth
still smoldering burnt
as for gold at the end of a rainbow
my beast loses nerve and broncos me
off with a shirking coward's innuendo
sprawled out and busted
and choking on muck
in three inch deep mud puddle sludge
the battle feels lost and the errand a
fool's labor wasted
on dream induced drudge
yet up to a knee
I rise from that muck
as I sense a surge buzzing nearby
but black lightning ballets at a speed
devil quick in a hue
out of range of the eye
my chase has no chance
my strategy flawed
the unbottled-yet bolts
out of reach
I abandon the hunt
and move without thought
like a tide trickles slow up a beach

only then as I wander directionless
free from the need to self-justify turns
I'm suddenly seized
by a shock of adrenaline
equal parts sizzles and burns
the moment exists out of time as I bask
in a clear yin-and-yang
comprehension
as I feel the unfelt and hear the unsung
halfway 'cross the Styx
to a deeper dimension
/
before I can cross the jolt fast departs
gone to ground at einsteinian speed
my supernova white dwarfs
euphoria usurped by need
impossible to further dwell
longer at lower altitudes
or sun sent glow consent to after
lightening blessed beatitudes
thus the quest to scour the dark
with desperate scavenge appetite
and skyward gaze against the odds
in prayer for manna from the night
thus the tempt to compromise
with vices teasing magic-lite
and habit haunt strange alleyways
with anxious actions uncontrite

convinced of fated symbiosis
moved to arts by light untaught
the guidance of an alchemist
as last resort I desperate sought
swearing secrets kept til death
techniques to the tomb concealed
I summoned bold that lightning black
that big bang origins revealed
/

for the pleasure of a permanent surge
for the thrill of a dynamite charge
the reverb of gold notes choir sung
and the lingering taste of truth
charred on the tongue
because the descent
is a scene uninspired
a reflection routine
for beat monks mind retired
black lightning alone
proves my night-prescribed med
wine divine fed from breast
for the Bacchian-bred

carl's open mic

Samaritan Sam
holds the door as I enter
with a reverential bow
that's not exclusive
he's what I call a panhandle dissenter
running an arthouse hustle unintrusive
any meal any time
as the time only counts
for Dalia who close counts the change
and Henry big Henry
who rows with his mop
like a seeker of sane
up a river of strange
the lights never dim
and the door never locks
at Carl's Open Mic extravaganza
where the locals can loiter
and hatch their revolts
out of mind on east end of the plaza
you can keep
your Pinecrest Diner crowd
they've nothing off menu to say
a woman just asked for my Cheetos
but I'm Cheeto-free to her dismay

Henry spies and wakes a slumping
dozer with a shoulder poke
"How long you gonna nurse
that cup of coke?"
mumbles about a refill
Henry laughs and walks away
"You been slurpin' nut but melted ice
since yesterday!"
reunion of step-children
of step-children of the gold rush
concerned for city's sake
by Chronicle reports of bullpen woes
sifting for nuggets
still the sport of preference
though they'll settle
for the heatlamped hashbrown glows
I used to grab a chair
at the Moulin for over easies
before that a stool at the Lafayette
'til they got crooked out of the lease
but downtown diners
can't compete with Carl's
their scenes too savory and their grills
stew swamps of grease
bastion of burgers thick
backstories juicy
the taste of guess/the/city
wrapped in paper waxed and white

where confessions mix with
nonsense rant delusions
and the badge boys
keep the quarantine
and never drop in for a bite
the reggies rotate through
as streetwise instincts guide
migration
noon around the fountain like campfire
front page photo fodder
social reform adjuration
vultures poised for lunchtime suits
to rush retreat as breaks expire
but as the locals jostle
with the pigeons for the scraps
the badge boys watch
with heavy hassle stares
that chill the temperature
and corral the crowd back into Carl's
where Dalia leans on counter
while she waits on a call
from Old Navy
as a fourth-straight patron pays
all dimes
for an order of biscuits and gravy
and she slides him card number five
then hollers "seventeen"
and he figures he's bought some time

and asks the key to the latrine
Henry hands it over
wags his finger with a warning
"don't be thronin' in there
'til tomorrow morning!"
while the fuzz huddle at Philz
amid the hipsters
and resolve to fix the eyesore
long deferred
scheming over steaming cups
of Wonderbar
how to slyly trim the fat
and buffalo the herd
/
patrol car creepin quiet
with its lights off
rolls slow toward the gaggle
and they scramble in response
some hightail down the stairs
into BART station
while others flee toward
their safer haven fastfood sconce
inside they dive to alibi booth tables
or like a clown car bunker
pile in toilet hideaways
muses of modern San Fran
bandit fables
outlaw junkie 'cisco castaways

the black and white
shines spotlight into Carl's
then veers on 7th street
toward the 'loin
the siren wails and V8 engine gnarls
as nocturnals slip back out
to night rejoin
the open mic procedure flows informal
outbursts of interruption
fly like roses of applause
the thematic thread can span from
speech in tongues to paranormal
inspired rowdy libertines
in Carl's midnight mirage
as Dalia rolls her eyes and sighs
and asks if my mind's yet made
as Henry tries to sweep me
like the mess I am off the filthy floor
and the mad poet repenters sing
laments of renderments unpaid
as I stumble t'ward the exit
where Sam Sammy
opens wide the door

junkboat

orient of the east bay
main square named not for icon Lee
who fought the master Wong Jack Man
then spread the better story
legend wrung from oaktown fib in '64
but unifier Lincoln
who championed the railroad and
defended the immigrant's claim
honored here for that
more than the war
man spry seventy
handstands facing east
elbows braced stare steady heels high
against side pole of chin up bars
hears distant rhythmic patter drift
outdoors from social center
couple frisky eighty ping pongs well
worn paddles sharp as ever
feel faint gusts blow in off the bay and
straight up Harrison Street
woman monkish ninety zens on bench
by entrance shade of tree
prays on beads for children passing

Buddha souls and bouncing feet
grandfather creaky sixty pushes swing
with careful calloused hand
back bent from life of labor
perfect angle present task
nods to sidewalk hustling father
weary fifty late for work
who holds the door for father scruffy
forty huffing sweating more
younger sharp dressed thirty
watches from high window
sips from can of protein boosted tea
restless/ craving/ envious
of priceless family hindrances
spies across the way
hip girl twenty spraying art
paints a golden dragon mural
overtop red dragon mural
faded chipped defaced
in decades since re-touched by brush
commissioned then on re-erected
after-earthquake wall
as part of new year's celebration
webster route parade
even mighty wild-eyed
fortune blessing dragons fade
/
the community jewel is a junkboat

anchored in permanent port
steering wheels spinning in vain
rope ladders and curving slides
spilling off all sides
three sets of sails of chain-linked wood
to tease the gentle breeze
toddler crew amok from stern to bow
here the heart of Panasiatown
beats proud
as the future always
sounds the preferred note
here what's come and gone
can peaceful rest
where saplings rise
out of remaining roots
atop the sails are fastened metal flags
formed to mimic flapping in the wind
painted once but blazoned
clean by sun
you'd have to strain
to notice what's been done
vandals in the night
dared scale the masts
and etched across the flags
some R.I.P.'s
markers for mateys
lost at sea mid-journey
whose futures once were notes

preferred as any
dragon drafts
denied the chance to fade
I eat my lunch
and squint to read the names

worn soles

soft tan leather stitched up tough
without a mark or scuff
high end brand and brand new feel
lacking only the box
shelf displayed side cowboy boots
of imitation snakeskin
mine to own for only eighteen bucks
you can getta sharp deal
at the Broadway Goodwill
but you better check the loop
for the holes
I walked outta there
with a near as new pair
strutting ten feet tall
on some worn down soles
/
where be the mysize feet for which
they first were brand new bought
do they pace a solitary cell
sentenced to regret and rot?
did they wake one night to a bad luck
moon and trip on a gordian knot
then sign their name to the "too soon"
page of obits the papers forgot?

/

I choose my town
as I choose my shoes
least for the function
and most for the flavor
I choose my path
like I choose my shoes
with compass of gut
and an absence of waver
I shrug off my chips
as I shoehorn the heels
I slip off my vest as I tie true the laces
I unhinge preconceptions
as I quick once brush the tips
and undress inhibitions
setting off for off grid spaces

/

my feet are not fond of these shoes
though the fit is snug
they blister with rebellion
though the insoles soft
like mounds of down
they ache and rub resenting
my feet have splashed
and puddle slopped
loose wrapped in rubber flips
cheap flopped
and felt exotic earthdirt

audit

shift beneath a heartbeat's weight
on leisure sunrise walks awash in sea
nymph kisses from the tide
my feet do not appreciate
this patent calfskin costume
or buy into their spit shined social aura
wistful for barefoot decadence
ingrained by grains of sand
on the beaches of
the southern 'sphere's Gomorrah
/
still I ride my goodwill wheels
on a roadtrip of wild capers
returning them to the likely scene
of their first life's after dark routine
my shoes march me to mischief
and justify my means
they tax write off my fishing trips
to burgundy midnight ravines
like a pair of sage crusaders
god-scheming my next conquest
they waltz me through wild tours
of the Larkin liquor stores
and hustle-step my heels
from O'Farrell's to New Century
nary a "by-your-leave"
nor a "mind the lowbrow entry"

night

like a scoundrel on a scavenger hunt
without aid of a list
I high-step through the old town
like a smut light nativist
and tap dance 'round the spills and
stains of Crazy Horse's joint
while California courtesans
starved clientele anoint
and all the while those rubber soles
they slide and scrape and slip
and lose a little tred with every step
as we graffitti in our wake
another soled out story
on a hell bent spiral nowhere route
that offramps short of glory
/
morning shrewdly intervenes
and I BART back to Oakland
emerging from the 12th street stairs
with a shirt cleaned shoe
in each beat hand
naked toes on cold concrete
apathetic to the stares
commuters eager to compare
my lack of lifestyle choice to theirs
the cashier looks them over/ shrugs/
returns them to the shelf
beside the still unbought

audit

still imitation snakeskin boots
I turn toward Ogawa Plaza
where worn soles rest easy
on tufts of green grass doused in dew
and wholesome to the roots

c. e. candidates

garden party atmosphere
in the penthouse suite
who's who rubbing whatnots
with the town car class elite
balcony with vaster view
than knew the ancient kings
a god type perch
for doing god damned things
down here on street level
there's a rally of some sort
speaker peddles promises
to status quo distort
buyers pay applause and time
for bargain discount hope
meds from feds dosed audibly
to social sadness cope
/
job posting for president
on craigslist U.S.A.
casual encounters page
election day soiree
/
double tongued big talker
wants to make decisions for me

says he's got the seasoning
and I don't got the time
tells me there's a plague
but good news! he's the remedy
as his toxic words
the breeze swept air begrime
lambs instinct from birth
to seek security from rams
while alpha wolves
compete to poach the sheep
to me roles of the pasture
seem a lot like cyclic shams
a sucker system
whole-sold on the cheap

/

job posting for president
democracy or bust
resumes irrelevant
lies beget from trust

/

three hundred million
nation population
can't come up with thirty-two
can play pro quarterback
the pocket gets too hot
under the pass rush
as the huddle plan for glory
turns to fortune flushing sack

the secret's not the scheme
but the contingency
the talent's not the arm
but the unflapping
the currency's the calm
in anxious instancy
the ideal package buddha mind
in herculean wrapping
the three cheered victor quarterback
risks all the dents and dings
while unauthorized biographers
expose his armor's every chink
but the O.C. in the booth
still gets to wear the golden rings
and knows the hero crystal
isn't worth the public clink
/
more dire is the "right stuff"
dearth in politics
blooper ballot listing
not one worthy white house resident
look like two bags of prunes
mislabeled trail mix
sound like snake oil salesmen
hawking hurricane-proof tents
where you wonder
went the best and brightest
well that penthouse was not built

to bunk the staff
why don't they show job interest
in the slightest
ceding instead to Sec. Macbeth
& Donald J. Falstaff
/
job posting for president
negotiable qualifications
stockholder discretion
subject to market fluctuations
/
chess board battle
played with checkered pieces
blemished dollhouse stand-ins
for the queens
donor dinners influence increases
as shadowed fingers
string the figurines
crowded there
behind the drawn-closed curtain
those best & brightest
make their bankrolls rain
calling plays
without regard for rulebook
as campaign donated strawberries
fizzle their champagne
debate duel set for live-action
aristocrats

dirty joke turned comic tragedy
bonfire of insanities of plutocrats
e pluribus unum atrophy
/
job posting for president
moth tendencies preferred
'fore the spotlight's bright
and never dims
center stage in this theater
of the absurd
/
job posting for president
on craigslist U.S.A.
casual encounters page
election day soiree

cupcake prime

moist tastes the moment
warmth perfectly
for an instant pouched
crucible of feasting rituals
head-on hilltop charged
rating scent not same as sight
not same as bite
not same as chew
not same as gulp
not same as sweet contented fullness
not important
pleasure eaten
not the point
consumption not defining
does not validate but witnesses
though often failing even that
tardy and craving pang distracted
life focus askew
/
pillage the cupboards
fill the bowl
nothing missing matters
method matters in the mixing

matters mucho the mixing
oven knob turned tepidly
to recipe degree
however not all handiworked the same
not so new so brand
so knob turned random
guided by god hand
same that gathered 'gredients
same that churned the congress bowl
same will hold in palm
baton of blame
or try to pass it on
/
flavor's fete the lifespan of a spark
the textured richness of a dream
wings of a soaring peregrine
gone before celebrated
first the fetus bakes
and existentialists retort
existed as stuff tucked on shelves
existed then as soupy fudge
exists still same and too anew
inspired into bloom by blitzing heat
rises from its form fit cup
ambitious & rebellious
rises observed through oven window
rises unrestrained untinkered with
rises yet at mercy of the hand

/

straight outta tray perspective
shape restrictions gone unnoted
until rapid expanse spilling out the top
and splaying slowly crawling
as young babe escapes a blanket
as old snake escapes shed skin
suggesting further spread potential
optimism plumes
as the moist moment approaches
as the oven door jerks slight ajar
for peeking as the toothpick lunges
like a spartan's spear

/

wince once and take the splinter probe
the timer can't be trusted
timer just an average of a precedent
not prescient
oven window blurred and inconclusive
visual a shroud report
toothpick pierces top
with light resistance
true to center mass
then quick to calibrated tongue
attuned to tell the difference
between
"almost there" and "done"
as the chemistry keeps churning

as the knob remains in place
/
lost in fortune's foliage of growth
oblivious to eyes and pick
reveling in the heat
irrelevant the knob
the source
the process origins
the recipe
(all lists are limitations)
best abandoned unconsidered
no "coulda been a muffin" speeches
nothing to be gained
no notice of the others thriving
likewise geminis sharing the tray
no crisis of "i cupcake" self
in light of grand scheme
food chain revelations
/
prime an apex-pointed peak
with width barely for toeprint stance
the altitude allows no chance
for balance across time
thug bouncer winds patrol
for vagrant lingerers
and each preceding moment
fits the climb
each following the fall

but ever slightly fate suspends
the second when the moisture
crystallizes flavor
pulsing evenly throughout
backbeating fleeting genesis
of soft deliciousness
existing outside obligation
being pulsing without whispered
fetishes to be a meal's dessert
/
baker's dozens
born from shortchanged budgets
many mixed in troubled haste
as many overbaked unsupervised
then dumpster tossed
offenses of aesthetic
past the peak no reverse route
chief inquiry elusive or incumbent
whether every cupcake
truly every single cupcake ever baked
no matter sugar brand
no matter heartiness of mix
no matter model oven
or attention of godchef experienced
that summit glory moment
emanating fresh but unindulged
i say oh yes!
they do

they must
she did
she must've
even she
oh yes! even hard-shelled she
was once upon a time
exquisite prime

black hawk blue

midnight
corner
Hyde & Turk
clipped pigeons strain their ears
trespassing padlocked parking lot
brown paper bags of pounder beers
riffraff crowd of busted cars
lame ponies without owners
praying for piano bars
from long gone jazz ghost donors
and I'm vibing kind of blue
kind of a greenish hue of blue
as we wait here for Bill Evans
full moon & cigarette lit seance
waxing once upon a neon
once upon a scene
waiting for Bill Evans
and his ivory boned machine
/
sidewalk plaque X marks the spot
monument for moment lost at sea
flotsam legends scattered
to four corners
jetsam jams adrift

amid the 'loin antiquity
notes which soared like cannonballs
from horns that wailed and whined
intoxicating eardrums
as they downtown hip defined
devil-tailed tunes out backdoor slipped
to vice mischief incite
in alleyways they rollick yet
soundtrack of San Franciscan night
/
sign on chain link claims "lot full"
sold out show this evening
but I see only we
in the bulldozed Black Hawk's shadow
waiting here to hear Bill Evans
to assure us that tomorrow
when we're all a flat grazed parking lot
tour posters faded & faces forgot
erased from lit marquees
with the same effortless ease
that Bill Evans rolled a riff
with those key-tickling fingers
the song we sounded in our prime
after our time still lingers
when our Steinways sell for firewood
and snares for credit pawned
our legacies will keep the beat
like encores from beyond

moonlight on sourdough

the cannibal collective
has no appetite for light
they cower in the refuge of the shade
in caves and holes and under rocks
they hang and crawl and coil
abstainers from the break of day
parade
creeping quiet
'cross the evening esplanade
more like Mohican trackers
than a marching time brigade
confidants of casual discretion
stock brokers in the after hours trade
scavenging the gutter joints
'til morning
surviving on the scraplings
they bestow
confessions lost
amid the melting candle wax
moonlight spread on top of sourdough
/
she likes a breeze with a bit of a bite
a night with a full set of teeth

a pour to the lip of the rim
clean and neat
a stool with a rung for her feet
a crowd of anonymous samples
a room draped in shadows
and frugally lit
barbacks & keeps
well rehearsed to their role
quick on the refill
& sparse with the wit
a Tuesday night evening
that ends with a story
though not one to tell or to show
guilty pleasures served on diner china
moonlight spread on top of sourdough
/
she cross-legged sits
and drinks
and waits
and feels the evening's eyes
senses the beast encircling
as the jukebox sirens and sighs
the night plays not the part of prey
it cannot be hunted or chased
the night feeds on the hour grey
indifferent to hunger's haste
content to nonchalant advance
bait taken late & slow

audit

risk written in the recipe
moonlight on sourdough
/
the City scene shrinks by the weekend
like a cotton dress drowning in steam
from the Mission to North Beach
she back floats
staying one stroke ahead of the stream
a cursed avatar of the ancients
damned dame-ification of Nyx
goddess carcass
for vultures late craving
a flesh and bone nocturnal fix
the savage who claims her for feasting
will find that the meal's sin pro quo
as is the way for the witching
moonlight on top sourdough
/
there's Bob's sweets shop
on Polk street
the Pinecrest on Geary and Mason
and a dozen sleaze motels and havens
flop housing the vampire nation
every Joe present's a poacher
and half the Janes posing are Joes
by six when the Sutter dives open
the pickings are slim
as the stem of a rose

night

they sound retreat
to booths inside of Ace's
fixing bayonets
to meet the morning's charging glow
guts growling
short the ordered satisfaction
moonlight spread on top of sourdough

detroit ed can't decide

three fleet week boys at Heinold's
play the card game "first queen buys"
spilling much as sipping
hoppy tap-poured Racer 5's
discoursing on the finer points
of sea-legged popeye theory
whether dames are merely
diamonds in disguise
beneath the clock with frozen hands
detroit ed can't decide
as his past steps bags and all
into the bar
to meet the eyes and shake the hand
and buy a round of highballs
or turn his back
and peace of mind retain
recalling mother's wisdom
as he overhears the sailors
that a dust storm's
just a dirty diamond rain
/

they howl and bark toward the moon
and stumble out into the square
but cannot see the sky beyond the
lamplight halos 'round their heads
without the stars to steer a course
back to pin-ups and pillows
planked benches on the boardwalk
serve as til-the-bugle beds
watching them from Heinold's door
detroit ed can't decide
if a moment should pleasure defer
to moments still to come
as a hint of saxophone
drifts through the port front's salty air
or if each minute living
is a diamond from Time's mine
a priceless jewel to be revered
as one of a kind rare
its carats left uncounted
and its details uncompared
voraciously indulged
despite a value undeclared
/

the predawn feeding flock of 'gulls
squawk early reveille
so the mermen
with their cottonmouths
arise and readjust dress whites

audit

rushing 'fore the anchor weighs
with alibis aligned
already scheming for the next port's
liberty delights
waving them a bon voyage
detroit ed can't decide
as he bends toward a cola can
discarded on the ground
if diamonds need not only light
but awestruck eyes to gleam
or if they shine
before they're even found
as sight unseen beyond the sunrise
still sparkle those distant stars
and deep beneath a fresh tattoo
there yet resides the covered scars
/
statue
back to
orange whales of ships
& whitewashed cargo cranes
posed mid-gesture point unfinished
argument unpunctuated
audience dispersed
replaced by morning walkers
and their wolves far too domesticated
would not recognize the wild
or dare to answer if it called

standing before Jack Griffith London
detroit ed can't decide
as he spits and with his jacket sleeve
wipes clean the figure's
bird shit crown
if the polish on the bronze
improves the lustre
if sauvignon blanc white wine
improves the oyster
if cut and set on solid gold
improves a precious stone
if forever is a promise
anyone can buy to own

no meter sunday morning

autumnal winds
rush roar gust scoot sweep past
martinique blue Pontiac
firebird trans effing am
golden dust caked cali plate
nineteen hundy seven eight
easy breeze waves break 'round
wash splash
rusting middle aged and aging muscle
oxidizing dream machine
built to last but vain are plans
and expectations bluffing hands
gto tires turned kiss curb
facing downhill view of Fillmore
quote-unquote needs
scrub wax paintjob tune-up
oil change and full tank fill-up
don't we all but not today
no meter sunday morning
/
qualifies for classic plates
even unpolished these chrome curves
don't pay for car show lingerie
o.g. status evident

truth is in the tired tread
never trailer shackled pick-up hauled
not 1 night jail garaged
red arrowhead westward aiming
windows rolled a crack
tufts of smoke billow out
rising like signals to the tribe
west coast war parties like to lose
the "war" part on the weekends
passengers brain e-braked
neurons placed in park
no traffic on the mind's highway
no meter sunday morning
/
survivor snails who still remember
Manzanar internment camp
crawl-scale hill hemp bags slow towing
forward leaning
eyes to sidewalk half step half slide
no side glances
city seasoned
shock long since absorbed no
trepidation city salted
to each their own their space
no matter starting gate
regardless race
city livin' culture compromises
embrace the intermingling

when hot happenstance arises
covet not thy neighbor
nor prejudice presume
no cameras in the laundry room
no meter sunday morning
/
peace plaza pagoda
benches stained by wildlife staking out
for crumbs from couples
huddled crouched
on steps splitting takeout
chewing quickly moment spoilt
vibe unfit to frame as memory
too grizzly to gloss over
like a two day stubbled chin
as it should be no in-ranks inspection
stand sit lay recline
in pontiac at coma-toasted ease
no space reserved no V.I.P.'s
no meter sunday morning
/
a momentary planetary amnesty
to contemplate the golden gate
multi-lane mirage
insurance schemes cash out beneath
on faulty trampolines
in drifts Pacific mist armada
Francis Draking everything

Presidio to Fillmore
laying coat of dew
on firebird martinique blue
pontiac trans effing am
all day autopilot
no hassle lights no rearview checks
no beatdowns or beat down protests
no meter sunday morning

below broadway

there you are
pinned in space
another half drawn crayon star
stationary fool waiting on winning
don't you know
the real ones don't stop spinning
motion stokes the magic of the burning
don't you know
the real ones were born churning
no credit counting revolutions
half-way through the turning
don't you know
that time is ever-bending
proofed both non-existent
never-ending
your perfect manicure inspires pity
lotioned palms unscarred
by blister's sting
fleshy calves accustomed escalators
stuck now stranded broken elevators
hard to blame a button for not blinking
pointless pointing finger at an arrow
don't you know

the way out's right behind you
stairway to the reed fields
for the pharaoh
screech swift trains along the rails
clack high heels the career chase
wail brass horns old buskers hustling
silent as suspended thought you wait
registering no detected decibel
pile of clown clothes
painted tears to match
remember how hellbent
full head of steam
plunged cocksure into rapid stream
eroded now a pebble imperceptible
someday a single microscopic sand
do you struggle with the pivot
or the swivel
grease the joints with guts
instead of nerves
did you get all of the 'rithmetic
you need
do you figure odds of failure
cannot odds success exceed
no guarantees of what waits
on street level
possibly effort wasted
on an errant steered pursuit
the crucible of steps

ensures no payoff
sound retreat
there's not a slide to chute
ever see a butterfly
hanging on a twig
when first he climbs reborn
out of cocoon
how's he know the hour's safe
for exiting
how's he know its time
and not too soon
how's he know what
fancy new wings do
that when he first leaps
will not tragic fall
the secret of the butterfly's
he doesn't know
just trusts and risks
and flaps against the flow
don't see a lotta butterflies in Oakland
seems like a lot of caterpillars though
lamenting as the yellowed leaves
keep falling
clinging to creaking branches
mid the throe
how's that freedom sandwich taste
you scraped up off the floor
how long ya think it's been there

gettin trampled
do the notes of piss
pair well with zinfandel
do you wonder if handmade
is any healthier
is the elevator coffin not depressing
is the cityscape not picturesquely vast
are you still the type
who curls up in a fantasy
and rents out mind's raw present
to a rose-highlighted past
can you recollect
what sizzling sunrays feel like
the charge of wind
and wet thrill of fresh rain
not tired of this greenhouse
full of concrete
phosphorescent tan session
while waiting for your train
blurry smeared resemblance
on twin dividing doors
blinking back at you with quiet blame
or is it you all smeared and blurred
staring at a door
that's conscience clean
mind-fibbing a campaign alibi
flexing all your muscle
to force an unbought smile

audit

root rotted once-inspired inclination
determined to never leave
the twelfth street station
unsure if you are real or a reflection
lucidity fragmented
by flickering faulty lights
waiting on a promise
out of service
fists in pockets
clenching figment rights

myrtle & gallows

i the island illusion
space wasting pace interruptor
collector of coins paid for karma
best of intentions corrupter
possessions in piles of debris
sprawled putrid corpse worn for worse
social reject gutter-exiled
hitching for a ride backa hearse
i the island uncharted
stain of an obstacle gallows & myrtle
artfully high-stepped
in perfectform stride
by equestrians seasoned to hurdle
no more of a hassle than muttshit
just a messier smudge to unsmear
forgotten before the next corner
plight mirage that'll soon disappear
i the island deserted
littered with remnant regrets
messages scattered unbottled
dreams in drift piles of forgets
stopover on passage to nowhere
volcanic mistake out of place
awaiting the shift change vixen parade

audit

leaning 'gainst wrought iron lace
punctually prompt
past the playground they sway
congeniality muses for pay
navigating the puddles of me
with catwalk-blistered steps
pushups pumps props in fat purses
false faces already applied
crossing the street to New Century
where they slip through a door
on the side
i the island habitable
with elbowed bridges flexbent
suspensions of faith for the transient
last resort of the portless percent
weakened at joints from disappoints
to mid-life disrepair
sagging and swaying
on verge of collapse
in the Tender's evening air

rain stance

sunlight stales quick
on palates seasoned
clear blue skies
like Sunday conversations
i celebrate the rumbling approaching
church bells for the dark clouds
rapid closing
plant bare feet in field
of 'lions tumbling
open arms to Pickett winds
encroaching
rain not gutpunch welcomed wincing
when no gust affecting angle
chilling droplets as they splash
when you don't have balls to get to
shallow impress to abash
wind not wicked hinderance
steed team pulled Zeus chariot
siren songs filled courage sails
spirited man's conquest fails
sheriffed seasonal shift changes
whispers truth i skeptic listen
mind surfing the skyline's rigid spine

time not figment fabrication
voodoo trick or parlor game
beast beyond our whip to tame
steady star heavenly poled
luminating mirror's frame
mother dream remembered
hollers warning
turning i see edge of field
running free with childish glee
reaching
realize
not tree but she my refuge
arms transformed branch armaments
vita patronum protectoris
/
pre-dawn present searching city still
samba queen Sumatra
dressed to dance
between lake and Lakeshore Drive
my slab of lakeside solace
Reginald in shadows cloaked
behind a lamppost pillar
joggers pacing huffing
creaking counting laps
self-medicated penance
for self-inflicted regrets
i wanna be cool casual
as those can't be bothered egrets

as nonplussed in my standing
as their staying
Reggie postures protest
of my presence
resents ambitioned stasis
abandons hideout turning to the street
grumbles unkind futurist predictions
after a pause i slide into his spot
behind the lamppost pillar
in the shadow's envied dark
look down and cannot see my shoes
gaze west across the water
neon Tribune straight ahead
the sun somewhere behind my back
less than hour rising
then the thunder bass drum pounds
intros unforecast storming clouds
like hoodlums creeping ambushing
cracking quiet-splitting sounds
turn to check on Reginald
cowering back to covered nook
front gone diner left of Lucky's
occupied he turns returns
desperately exposed
and in full open field retreat
toward the unroofed
pigeon painted concrete
where bad luck lightning threatens

and he sees no tree but me
watching the frightened egrets flight
yet unimpulsed to flee
branch-bestowed
by default beside him
our backs against the lamppost pillar
betting on the race
between the lightning and daylight
waiting to see which ruins
the placid chill of night
so it is as so it goes
somes your role the Reggie
times instead the Oak
enchantingly at mercy
either way of Chance's stroke

mocha for musa

the African horn blows ancient blues
as sandship pirates
pillage shores for hobby
second cousins Musa's since forgotten
as he scans the quiet
midnight hotel lobby
Eritrean jackpot green card lotto
first flight one way trip to SFO
knew soon as silver plane took off
the "good" part of "goodbye"
to be reborn a phoenix gotta fly
/
thirty ninth west Telegraph in Oakland
downtown Asmara relocated scene
advertising "Ethiopian" cuisine
all-male crowd with eyes
fixed on the flat screen
watching La Liga derbies
live from Spain midweek midday
then park bench convo afternoons
light naps tri-habitated rooms
evening en masse commute
out of MacArthur

audit

security guard graveyard gigs
pay fourteen bucks an hour
/
Musa's teflon sunny mood
self manifests
does not dark cloud consider
when deciding clothes to wear
disinterested in news reports
tone deaf to their tabloid despair
forgives the police hassle
when mistaken profiled local
no good time female chasing
bachelor budget patient pacing
watchers whisper wagers
predicting the fast won't last
that Man's ambitions
always lead to vice
but Musa takes that cold
leftover pizza slice
from the front desk dick
with gracious gratitude
savoring each cheezy morsel chewed
/
morning shift end celebration
pilgrimage to Webster street
Musa's gotta sweet tooth
for a mermaid
potion mixing

sweet-tailed
emerald muse
mother of exiled
modern wretched refuse
Lady Liberty of twenty-first century
patriotically aroused by the aroma
recalls each time
the first time scent seduced
steps beyond the immigration shuffle
where officer with face
he can't remember
offered only silence
with that golden-plated stamp
but the brilliant young barista
swami cafe cognoscenti
read his thirsty soul
and suggested mocha venti
then when he uttered "Moses"
by a miracle misheard
despite pronunciation
careful rehearsed on the bird
marker scribbling "MUSA"
hastily on side of cup
like some Ellis Island registrar of yore
metamorphosis completing
for the new-named Eritrean
who first sipped the taste of freedom
from her pour

epochal whir

legend making truish story
early june of sixty four
laying live 'Right Now' recording
san fran bebop
broadway Workshop
moanin' out the sweat
fronting fresh improv quintet
meditating mid riff over bear sized
e.h. roth carved bass
black bullwhip loose coiled by his stool
emanating genius icon cool
/
loud metal fan relief whirring
barkeep pulls plug kills the buzz
mingus lika grizzly beestung roars
reaches for that braided hide
while the snare ratatats that beat
cracks it lika master tamer
saxophones wail through the heat
hollers "that boy's in the band tonight!"
barkeep turns a scarlet shade of white
rushes to reverse the sin
bullwhip drops to floor

fat fingers return to strings
falling in flow seamlessly
as to Ming Kong
the brass and drums defer
strumming off the treble of the whir
/
moon compassed unto the breach
lost in maze of slopes
alleyway spelunking north beach
censusing the saintly
punk monk popes
paranoid that concentration
means 'right now' discrimination
complimenting details lost to crop
ham bone flavor
siphoned from the slop
/
strutting street prince
passes me on sidewalk
tunes from his mini boombox
scratchy soar
profane truthtalk poetry
with hiphop heartbeat score
old me instinct cringes at the noise
hopes his duracells die
or a downpour radio destroys
now me envies
grand scheme recognizer

wise gets it modern Mingus realizer
knows song is just a part
of moment's soundtrack
enhancing and enhanced by
live surrounding singing scene
the coot chirp horn beep
heel step child weep
even haunting humming
from the phantom fan's ghost whir
no bouncer by the mind's backdoor
soundwave sans segregation
washing over us
as one orchestral stimulation

diners de la loin

the sunday slandered sugar salesman
sweets seducer knuckle knocks
public lynched for peddling pleasure
discount deals on last year's stocks
not by devilish design
no sin of thine
there is no sin
concept unneeded
contradict'ry
in this murky muddled world
of justice blinding juries
worse than useless
interfering
petition passed to blow the noose
house
out with crime with wrong with rules
i'm too busy digging blues
to find something to blame
for this cyclic epidemic
highway jacking Life's good name
bottle necking two laned hearts
with joy jam route remorse
not counting corner born of course

why include them now
this lament is dedicated
to the leisure inundated
high on cardboard pedestals
robed in rented medals
crowned with inherited laurels
waving to wild clapping crowds
of propaganda murals
not even certain which event
they've labeled an accomplishment
too preoccupied with planning
private island parties
to consider if the race
ease won ran fair
as their offkey "hail the victor"
anthems blare

/

culture quilted fiber optic
virtu digits touching
full bloomed false realities
age of metawareness
short-circuiting the System
so was the cave art algorithm
drawn with naive rock chalk
under fire's supervision
i hopeful went a-hunting once
for my kindreds birth assigned
for the clubhouse of my "generation"

meaningless as citizen
back to "us" and "them"
back to you and i
to the social classless ball
with six billion cinderellas
in a line to share a gown
ragged fraying hand me down
waiting for a waltz
tokened for a karmic break
with an eye-patched eunuch prince
whose crown looks hella fake
/
gold flaked globe of earthen clay
molded by the diners
in their portrait airbrushed image
first one opened on day seven
breakfast all day ever since
every order over easy
originality deep buried under mound
of neuron smothered butter
sparks of spirit syrup doused
before the flames can fan
boy scout badged consumers
carry license to critic
insisting on a private booth
with off-the-menu perks
waiting on promotions
from short order sterilizers

to maitre d positions
as the Q.C. supervisors
/
suckers wait on walk-in seats
idealists in the cue
polys mathing prices
as their appetites accrue
money just a slick card trick
frugality for fools
life a smorgasbord buffet
comp included with your stay
and if you don't believe me
ask those ducks
now waddling out the door
guts bulging wallets none the lighter
smirks of satisfaction
as they after smoke re-enter
granted taking seats
in absence saved
venn diagramming
same ambition scheme
alpha apeman fantasy
the diner owner dream
not to build or plan or run
but front door keys possess
name in cursive neon 'cross the top
blinking beacon visible
from freeway after dark

the less endowed and denim gened
burn for nametags gloss engraved
aspiring to apologize
for service past depraved
spiral down the row of stools
to dwindle hopes of busboy shifts
eight hours without sitting down
for copper Lincoln tips
remarkable the never-dying
ever-churning hope
remarkably incapable
of puncturing sky porcelain
with avant possibility
peering periscope
centrifugally chained
by the circus yin and yang
rotating through the roles
with hushed harangue
/
let's revolutionize the soda fountain
hasta la free refill para siempre!
replace the soap with sanitizer
brand name hot sauce bottles
between the Heinz twin models
crayon painted curly straws
to pacify the kids
if not these time pursuits
then what

appetizer entree two desserts
then what
mint chocolate milkshake
with a chocolate mint cake
at what point does appetite
mid-meal crisis question
both the why behind the hunger
and the what beyond the taste
balance found in
between-feeding comatose
instead of clifftop yoga
on the California coast
after feast digest reflection
scraped and swept and wiped away
with the life's work dirty plates
deposited in rear door dumpster
one more satisfied customer
/
i see others out the window
not in line for seating
not hungry though they haven't eaten
stomachs stirring
with different sensation
the third result reaction
to seventh day creation
rebellious by their being there
deballasting the balance
not even with spray cans in hands

graffiting wall protests
lean-to lounging in the lot
existential satellites
orbiting off-grid
conscientious game defectors
artfully abstaining from their id
intentions as opaque
as the diner windows clean
to better see breathtaking scene
of moving sights
great distances removed
/
booth no better than stool or standing
beast no bruter than me
diner by default assumption
incapable of more conclusion
thinking same of one another
drag racing the crosswalks
sizing faith by footwear
priorities by posture
is there more not really sure
but consider the miraculous
random mutation of wings
grandchild untraced offspring
of butterfly fish fins
dry and feather downed for flight
to steady steer
and sweep above the surface

see the pel-i-can
dive to scoop some lunch
whose luck is less evolved
why no gifted wings for me
no glide to my awkward stride
walking nervous waiting for
when the peli dives for me
/
consider sun and moon as diners
producer of space power and
consumer of warmth created
combustor of all energy and
reflector of energy's light
cook and counter side house reg
in their rays and beams we bathe
seeking purpose laden guidance
laying guilty pleasure fault
what of the lostboy loiterers
who do not reverential kneel
nor raise their eyes to recognize
and give no thanks for harvest
never asked for uncollected
what of the distant polished stars
where in their subtle shining
did our fathers first spy revelations
folklore explanations
plotted in the constellations
universal answers

night

**wrapped in a riddle coded ruse
teasing ancient
undeciphered
anamorphic clues**

fossilized frames

vibrant virgin forest dawn
subtle splendor glow on tips of trees
as rugged east bay ranges roam
gold nugget color coated grizzlies
nonchalantly as Gaea intended
with top of food chain tempered
regalese
/
sea otters and Ohlones
gather by their long shared shore
to meet the missionaries
anchored like conquistadores
crossed crusader warrants
painted 'cross sails
billowed by the breeze
/
thirst and lust as northern stars
guide ships of salt souled seafarers
who dive from decks to Barbary dens
then wake headached
on outbound crews
shanghaied for per scalp commissions
by the skid row sleaze
learning to say "syphilis" in Cantonese

/

John Q. Law Jack Manion
mick who scrubbed the North Beach
Black Hand clean
convenes the dragon families
silk talking warring clans serene
keeps the peace among the Tongs
until they learn to sleight of sight
their Sunday sermon
sentenced wrongs
placating Town Hall diocese
teetotaler trustees

/

black panthers in shades and berets
prowl patrol the people's placid lake
social unrest stoking
while inherent right invoking
a call to arms committee
like lynch mobs of San Franciscan lore
vintage vigilantes
from a hundred years before
open palm to compromise
replaced with raised clenched fist
threatening to civic power seize
quoting equal parts
Sun Tzu and Socrates

sumday's lemma

postulate of whywehere
career of chalk rubbed temples
front of chaos scribbled board
Creator theorem boneyard
erroneously starting
with a "G" instead of "i"
far side of equals sign
aligning
opposite a question mark
now near rolls the juggernaut
judgement wheels
the sacrifice slow grinding
last thought epiphanizing
that the exit interviewer
waits to see hypothesis deduced
not the one in desperation done
but complete proof of self
who woulda guessed
the spirit winds
would want to see the work?
/
hydro eccentric reservoir
ran dry from drought of stimulation
power to the City was

without warning cut off
Larkin Street apartment building
which from he last month evicted
had no choice but to evacuate
the pay on-time types too
bodegas closed
and locked
and chained
diner grill sizzle gone silent
those with dummy parachutes
crowded aimless
over-occupying space he previous
had thought ample abundant
waiting and degenerating
exponentially toward the sum
of importances and meanings
loose interpreted
from fuzzy mathed fib fairy tales
bedside lulla-lied
/
bush suite beats the Geary slope
construction there starts early
but Bill at Tommy's Joynt shares dope
the Haight is not so friendly
the only safe odds bet's the chill
which curling fetal less exposes
warmth a mind lie trick of will
coat pillow lined with roses

hope in nurtured roots
satisfaction in reflection
privileged class pursuits
far off course current direction
even all star schizophrenics
cannot simultaney-suffer
even online academics
cannot dream binary buffer
hunger now but only hurting
when compared to last week's feast
filthy habit state reverting
blame it on the bad luck beast
/
Midge the graveyard grifter
alley earner who clocks out at dawn
nocturnal resorter
on a no way out
migration route
well versed in the sumday song
and sings it like all nightingales
with whistling crescendo
audible from curbside car window
tractoring her patrons
with perfect pitched false notes
freak fantasy connoisseur
trained in night trade tricks galore
but once, many potholes before
leaned into theorem

chalk in hand
then as proof progressed
and fragile limestone
stick ground down
traded in the last of it
for one surrender drag
from a sympathetic cigarette
and glimpsed the final answer
escaping to star rafters
with the smoke
/
Huxley wrote we dig our graves
with mouths in glutton fever
if that's the case
Scant shoulda lived forever
instead of the immortal swingers
ever wanting it both ways
getting double pleasure pay
on perma holidays
Yeats of the streets
Market Street monk
found dead with stack
of rants and rhymes
in pocket folded forty times
haunts Javier the Catholic cop
who found him in pose of prostration
halfway down stairs to BART station
trampled by late-runners

audit

with cold muttered
"rest in peace"'s
leaving to interpretation
if the message lies
on worded lines
or in the creases